Sandall Park - Past and Present

Symeon Mark Waller

Scan this code for more Doncaster history publications

Written and compiled in recognition of the continuing good work of

The Friends of Sandall Park

www.sandallpark.org.uk

And with the help and support of the following supporters

There's **more** than one way to use **self storage**

When you're buying or selling a house, self storage is a **fantastic solution for storing** your household possessions. But did you know there's more to storage than moving house?

You may be fed up with all the clutter in your home and just want to give yourself more space. You could be having building work done or redecorating, with every room seeming to be in a mess and full of valuable items that could be damaged. Maybe you'd like to work from home or have a business based from home; you may need to clear a room to make an office or not have enough room to store equipment. You might need to clear space to rent out a room or find somewhere to put your winter wardrobe. You may run a local sports team and need somewhere to store the kit. The list is endless – we've seen all these reasons for storing and more.

Over 16,000 people can't be wrong.

Self storage from Ready Steady Store is the **affordable solution** to all of these problems. Prices start from as little as only £5per week. And it's flexible; there are over forty different unit sizes and you can store for as little or as long as you like. Plus with extensive security and PIN code access, you can come and go safe in the knowledge your things are safe.

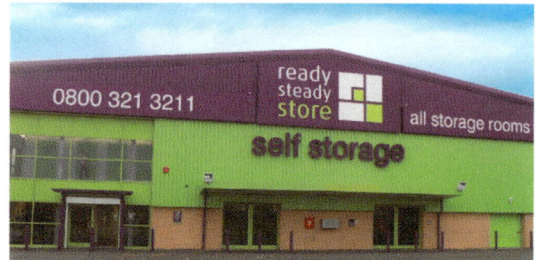

NORTH DONCASTER VILLAGES AN ILLUSTRATED HISTORY

SYMEON MARK WALLER

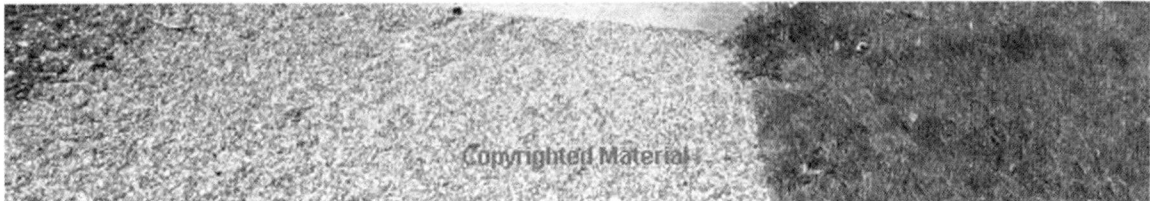

TWO ROSES

BREWED IN · BARNSLEY

BREWERY

ATTITUDE
PALE
ALE 4.3% ABV

American Pale Ale brewed in collaboration with Two Roses Brewery

LATITUDE BREWERY

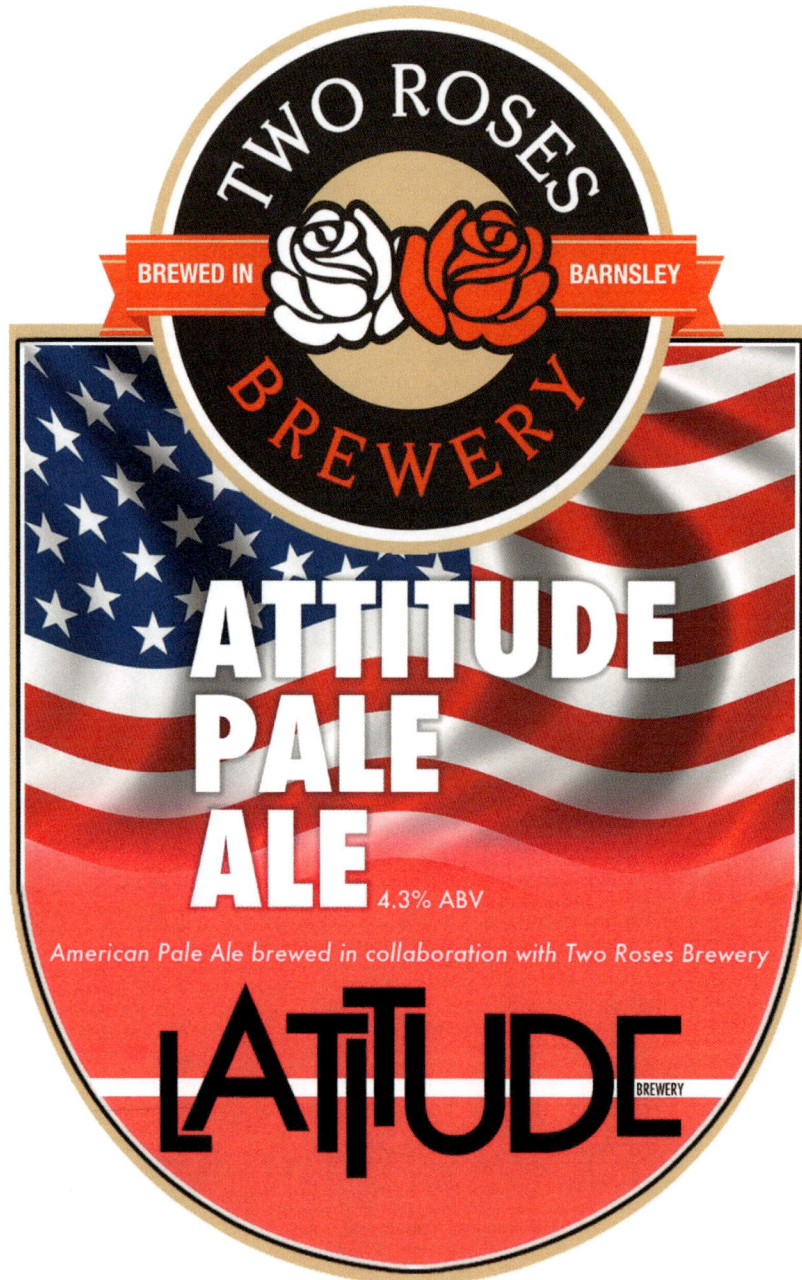

www.latitudebrewery.co.uk

Foreword

-oOo-

Over time Sandall Park became a genuine 'people's park' where visitors would travel to enjoy the boats, Peter Pan train, golf course and playgrounds. At its peak during the 1960's and 70's the park was one of Doncaster's most popular visitor attractions.

My childhood recollections of it were almost like a trip to the seaside. We'd pack a lunch and the whole family would set off from Intake to the boating lake, it seemed like miles. We'd spend the whole day there and play and picnic, happy days.

Alas, the early 90's saw a catastrophic decline in the parks fortunes and almost all attractions were removed. The next ten years saw the park decline even further.

The Friends of Sandall Park was created in 2003 and I became a member in 2004 and Chairman in 2005. Looking back at the 'good old days' I could not believe the decline in such an important asset and I could not help but imagine what sort of memories the present generation would have about Sandall Park. We created plans not only to reintroduce attractions to the park but to reduce crime and develop the infrastructure that would enhance the park for years to come. The challenge has been turning the plans into real action. Fortunately the group is focused on getting things done and not just talking about it!

With the introduction of playgrounds, picnic areas, sensory and nature trails, fitness trails, information boards and improved angling and toilet facilities my hope is that in the future park visitors will look back and see the current period as the 'good old days'.

Sandra Crabtree

Chairman - Friends of Sandall Park, 2014

Sandall and its Park

-oOo-

Introduction

When I was first approached to create a written document of the area we now call Sandall Park I was a little reluctant I have to admit. Through my interests in local history and my research into every kind of topic on that theme I had not yet discovered any useful material on Sandall and the area was just far enough out of my line of expertise that I had failed to see just how rich in history and heritage it was. I possess distant childhood memories of visits to the cafe and boating lake with my parents and siblings but those occasions were so rare that no real lasting imprint has been left in my mind.

The main reason for me deciding to take on the project was because of the good work of that locally famous community group The Friends of Sandall Park. 'The Friends' are a stalwart group of local people who have taken it upon themselves to improve Sandall Park for the benefit and good of the whole town. Their fine efforts have not gone unnoticed and a multitude of awards give testament to that fact. By far the greatest recognition to date came recently from Buckingham Palace when our Queen acknowledged the efforts of the group by presenting them with the 'Queen's Award for Voluntary Service', the equivalent of an MBE no less. The Friends, lead by Don and Sandra Crabtree, have a real enthusiasm that is quite infectious, and one which was immediately apparent at my first introduction to them. A lengthy discussion, followed by a tour of the Park, had me hooked on the idea of writing a book, not only to teach us of the past but to inform us of Sandall's evolution (with a great deal of intervention from 'The Friends') into a fantastic community asset.

I hope this book appeals to not only those of us that are interested in local history, but those that are proud of our surrounding so very much that it moves us to take guardianship of them and to protect them quite vehemently. In 2013, when I first put finger to keyboard, 'The Friends' are working hard to continually improve our experience at Sandall Park and long may this continue.

Symeon Mark Waller, Sprotbrough - 2013

Chapter One

-oOo-

Sandall and Wheatley Hills
A History

In his book, The History and Antiquities of Doncaster and its Vicinity - 1804, Dr Edward Miller writes on Sandall, "This village is two miles eastwards of Doncaster, and in its parish. The corporation of Doncaster has 1100 acres of land here, which is let upon an average at about twenty shillings per acre. The soil is generally a sandy loam, and the village inhabited by respectable farmers. Brick kilns are erected in this parish, from which Doncaster is chiefly supplied both with brick and tile. Sandall is pleasantly situated adjoining the River Dun, on which river here is a lock built for the conveniency of vessels passing and repassing." According to a Doncaster Museum publication written in the early 1970's, "..... there appears to be evidence to show that another Roman road ran from Rossington Bridge to Wheatley along the eastern side of Sandall Beat Wood to the bank of the River Don, at what is now the International Harvester's Factory, where a settlement of some kind is known to have existed, This road and its continuation northward to Barnsdale Bar may be the original Roman route to Castleford." If this evidence is still to be believed after more than 40 years have passed then it would place Sandall Park right on the edge of a Roman settlement. We already know that the fields that make up the area are ancient ones as it is clear they are of the 'ridge and furrow' type which was an ancient farming method allowing even the boggiest of soils to be cultivated. Modern ploughs are reversible whereas ancient oxen pulled ones were not. The continuous act of ploughing in circles meant that the soil turned in would form ridges (usually measuring one furlong ['furrow-long'] in length). This system can date the fields of Sandall Park to between post-Roman and the 17th century, they are almost certainly medieval.

Evidence of the ancient ridge and furrow farming methods can still be seen today

The area of Sandall must have been an important area immediately after the Norman Conquest for King William I saw fit for there to be an entry in his Domesday record. The record served the purpose of detailing all the lands that were held by the existing Saxon Lords who had governed Doncaster since the Romans left. The entry tells us that the area was owned by the Saxon, Skotakoll in 1066, but by 1186 it had been confiscated and placed under the protection of Nigel Fossard as a reward for helping to defeat King Harold at the Battle of Hastings. Fossard was a powerful Norman Lord who was placed in charge of 141 places throughout the whole of Yorkshire including the modern Bentley, Scawthorpe, Adwick-le-street, Hexthorpe, and Doncaster itself. In Sandall there were 4 pieces of woodland, two villagers, three smallholders and two freemen. There were three plough-lands having two plough teams. Neighbouring Long Sandall also had an entry, though one of far less significance. In Long Sandall there were three villagers and one freeman, the only difference being that the land there was held by Earl (King) Harold (King Harold held 843 places altogether from Lands End to Leeds with a high concentration in the Kent and Norfolk areas). William de Warenne, 1st Earl of Surrey, took over the lands under the new Norman rulership.

Domesday entry for Sandall ©Crown Copyright 2014

Apart from the Domesday entry and the official corporation documents on taxes and boundaries there is little information to be found that describes the Sandall area from before the 19th century, one has to wonder whether the better known Wheatley Hills has always distracted the historical writer's eye as there is much to be found on the latter. As Wheatley Hills is so very close to Sandall, in that it merges with it in places, I see no wrong in describing that area as a means of gaining some insight into the likely similarities between itself and Sandall. The name Wheatley Hills is somewhat of a misnomer as there are no real hills within its boundaries to speak of. One presumes that it derives its name from the fact that it sits on slightly higher ground, so much so that at one time, before the mass industrialisation of the Victorian era, one could allegedly see as far as Barnsdale Bar to the northeast and Retford to the south. Charles William Hatfield wrote in his Historical Notices of Doncaster, 1870, "A stranger visiting this point would experience disappointment, for the term 'Hills' is misapplied. The ground is a slight elevation from the surrounding country; but not as high and commanding as, in strictness, to bear that name." Hatfield goes on to describe the area's geographical location when he writes, "At the present day (1870) the 'Hills' begin immediately beyond the field that is attached to Green House (the Cumberland Hotel), and opposite the Wheatley toll-bar on the Doncaster and Thorne turnpike road. It is entered by a gate placed at the angle next to the road just mentioned, and where the Armthorpe road, diverted from behind Green House, runs from the turnpike. The road passes through a small belt of plantings, formed by Sir William Bryan Cooke, Bart., the first Mayor of Doncaster after the passing of the Municipal Bill. Beyond this planting, two roads diverge, right and left, and extend the whole length of the Hills. The upper road is the pleasanter of the two either as a drive or a walk. Proceeding along, you pass, on the left, a small clump of gloomy Scotch Firs, which were probably planted before the enclosures . . . . . towards the right on a slight slope, is Heather Wood, with the Gorsemeres extending to the Low Plantation, or Fox Cover, nearly adjoining the Red House. More to the right are the New Plantings and Intake farm, the property of W. H. Forman, Esq. of Pippbrook House. From this position there are also distinct views of the far-famed Doncaster race-ground, its Grand Stand, the Nobleman's Stand, and a long range of minor stands and booths. Yet further beyond are Rose Hill farm and the woods of Cantley, the property of John Walbanke Childers, Esq." The Wheatley of old was described as being covered in gorse with that spiked shrub forming the edging to the many drives that existed there.

This vantage point, similar to the aptly named 'Town View' at Scawsby Lees meant that armies of the past chose to set up camp there in preparation for their part in various historic battles. Certainly, General Wade's troops were encamped at Wheatley Hills before the siege of Pontefract Castle during the English Civil War. The high ground would undoubtedly have made the area around Sandall an attractive place to erect your tent and rest your blistered feet after a long days marching! I suspect that if ever Sandall Park underwent a thorough archaeological survey then there would be much to be found to remind us of its importance during those turbulent times of yesteryear.

Wheatley itself belonged to that long-standing aristocratic family the Cooke's, the seat being erected on land that became International Harvester's tractor manufactory. The fine mansion was sited thus so that a fine aspect could be had over Arksey Ings and Wheatley Park. Although the situation was idyllic, the land and the Hall itself was liable to flooding (on a regular basis) and so proved ill-placed, and latterly, little used.

And so, from the ancient descriptions given by Doncaster's historians of the past, we now have a fairly clear mental picture of Sandall and its immediate surrounding area. As we take a look at the enclosure maps of 1815 we are able to get a more accurate description of the brick and tile works together with the land that it occupied. The whole area that makes up the modern park once consisted of a number of separate fields owned by the Doncaster Corporation with private tenants in place. In that time the main fields were described as being "covered in pits, brickyard buildings and kilns," with a small plantation along the northeast edge and a sand quarry. The original brickyards took up more space than is now occupied by Sandall Park and there were clay pits and kilns to be found on the site now occupied by Shaw Lane Industrial Estate.

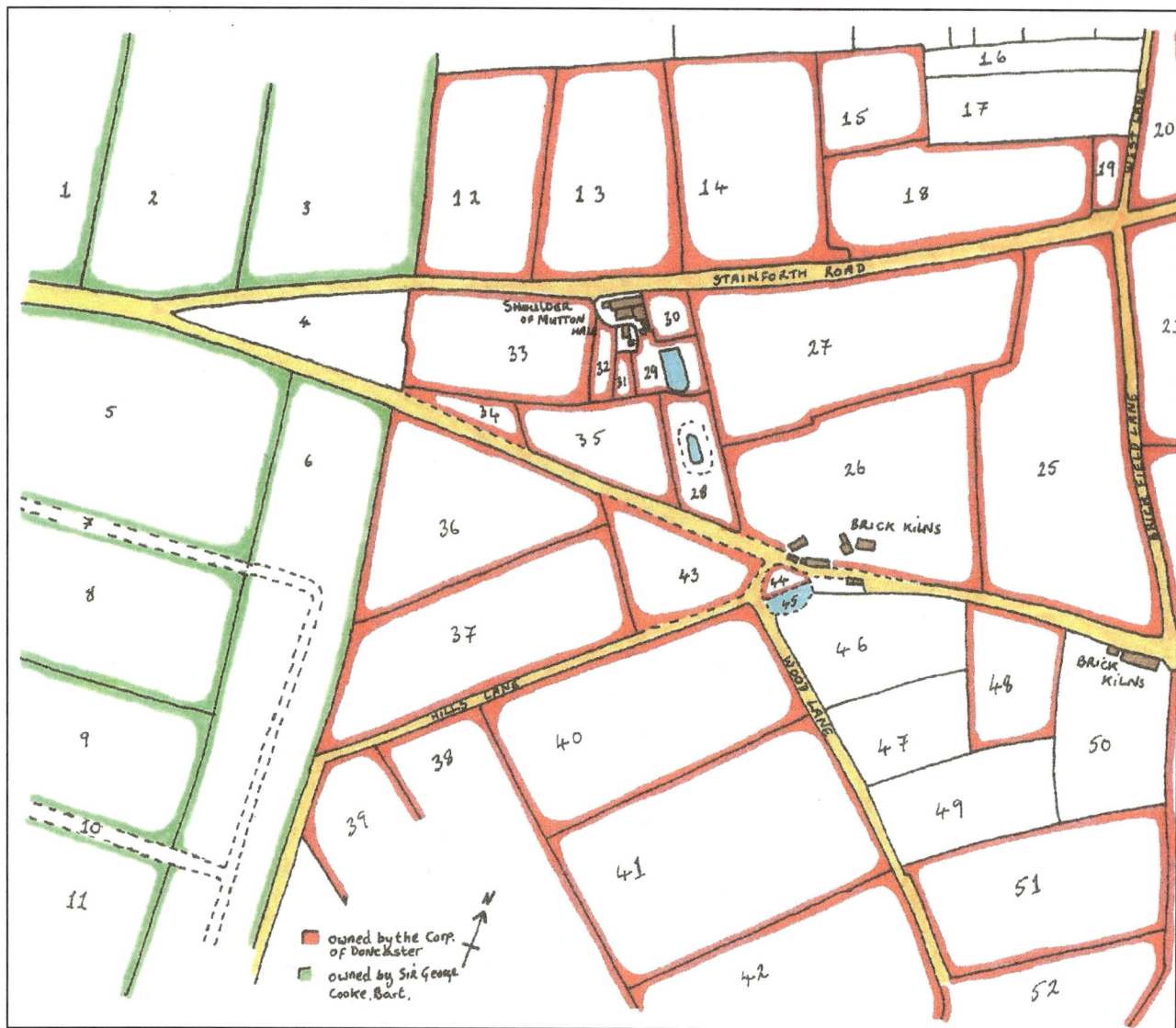

Revised version of the 1815 enclosure map showing Sandall Park within central triangle

Chapter Two

-oOo-

The Early Evolution of Sandall

As we further delve into the history of Sandall, a look at the 1861 entries illustrates how busy the site must have been during its heyday for there are recorded eight separate households containing thirty-three individuals under the heading 'Brick-Yards'. Joseph Senior is listed as the main employer, employing 24 men and boys; his occupation is recorded as 'Brickmaker' and the occupations of the inhabitants range from 'Brickmaker to 'Agricultural Labourer', demonstrating the importance of the area both for industry and farming. In the same census, Mr. Joseph Burns, a farmer of 250 acres at the neighbouring Streetthorpe estate (now Edenthorpe) only employed two farm labourers. How labour intensive must the brick making industry have been to have merited employing twelve times as many men?

As one skips through the subsequent census returns we see that by 1871 Joseph senior has either died or simply passed the running of the business down to his son Thomas. Thomas is married to a lady named Laura who was a local girl, being born at Armthorpe in 1841. Thomas and Laura had ten men and four boys in their employ as brickmakers. By 1881 Thomas was dead as was his eldest son Henry leaving Laura to run the brickworks single-handedly, save for the help of one or two servants. By now the brickyards were the home to forty individuals within 10 households. Finally, in 1891, Laura had left the Sandall brickworks altogether, presumably selling the business, as a new name appears in the census return and Laura is to be found residing at number 25, Queens Road, Wheatley with her two sons, William aged 21 and Charles aged 20. Her employment is recorded as 'living on own means' hinting at the fact that she has enough money to hand so as not to have to work. I have not yet conducted enough research into the possibility of this family being connected in some way to the Senior's of the Sandhouse, near Balby Bridge, the Sandhouse being that locally famous series of tunnels carved out of solid sandstone.
It certainly would be quite a coincidence if two families with the same surname were involved in the quarrying industry at such close proximity to one another in the same town.

Sometime between the 1890's and the 1930's, the brickworks ceased to exist and fell into dereliction and disrepair, so let us now fast forward to the year 1938, for this is the year that Sandall began its evolution into what we see before us today.

From looking at the Doncaster corporation minutes of that time we see that plans were underway to transform the former brick and tile works into an area for the community to enjoy. At a meeting held at the Mansion House on 4th August, 1938, the Parks and Cemeteries Committee, consisting of Councilor Ranyard (Chairman), Councilor W. Corbett (Mayor), Alderman Crookes, and Councilors E. M. Firth, W. Firth, Willins, Shaw and Trotter, discussed a report pertaining to Sandall Park. In that report they looked at various options for its future and different ways to make better use of the area. On the 23rd March, 1939, formal consent was given by the Minister of Health for the corporation to borrow £2,500 for works at Sandall Park and in April of the same year at one of these committee meetings a letter of reply was read out from the Ministry of Health "approving the proposals of the Town Council for the construction of the boating lake, boat-house and landing stage at Sandall brickyards." Various tenders were submitted for proposed road works and eventually, after some scrutiny, the one submitted by Messrs Frank Haslam Ltd. of Doncaster was accepted. In August of the same year it was decided that fishing should be allowed in the Park and further tenders were then invited for the construction of a paddling pool and a bandstand. In 1940, suitable fencing was bought and installed along the Thorne Road frontage and Messrs C. Massarella and Sons, of Doncaster, were granted the sole right to sell their ice-cream within the Park. After this, the improvements came in quick succession. By far one of the main attractions at the Park, and one that remained the primary reason for visiting right up until recent times, was the introduction of pleasure boats which were available to hire on the lake. On the 7th May, 1940, quotations began to be accepted for the supply of boats and it was recommended that £50 for five second-hand boats be paid to a Mr. A. Hoyle for them, in addition to these five boats a further four boats were hired from a Mrs. Otley, at the cost of £1 per week. The part-time attendant, Mr. Frost, who had been employed to look after Sandall Park would have been very pleased too as in June 1940 he received a 5/- per week pay rise while fishing tickets were reduced from 6d to 3d.

Chapter Three

-oOo-

Memories of Sandall and the Park
by
Margaret Frost

Sandall was a part of my life for many years, both before and after the Park came into being. My sister Val was three years older and my brother Michael two years younger than me. We were the children of Noel George and Mabel Frost. Noel was the younger son of George Edward Frost who lived at Sandall from 1931 to his death in 1956. Our much younger brother Tony was born in 1945. I've tried to put my memories in some sort of order. Some are about the family connection, others about the way the Park developed when seen from a personal point of view. We always called it Sandall, never Sandall Park or the Boating Lake.

My great grandparents, William Valentine and Sarah Maria Frost came to Doncaster from Fakenham, Norfolk, in early 1875, bringing with them their three children, the youngest being my grandfather George who was only a few weeks old. William had been a labourer and drayman at a brewery but came from an agricultural background. They lived in the Wheatley area, moving several times before settling on Wheatley Lane where most of the rest of their family of 14 were born. Sadly two daughters died in infancy.

William worked in the Wagon Shop at The Plant for a number of years but in 1895 he became a council tenant when he took over the defunct brickyards at Sandall. There were two cottages within the yard which were built in 1841 and William and his family moved into the one which stood on the site of the cafe that stands today. The living arrangements must have been a little cramped for the family so that at some point the need arose to extend the cottage, adding a kitchen and a small back room. Originally the property had only one living room containing a fireplace with a cooking range. There were two bedrooms, one at either side of the house, and a long, low scullery which had a window at one end and a door

leading out into the yard. The cottage had stone slab surfaces and no sink, water having to be drawn from a pump in the yard. I remember the living-room ceiling vividly for it was made of polished mahogany, and the oil lamps glowed as they reflected from it. The added kitchen had its own sink with cold water tap. Behind the cottage there stood a stable with a cobbled floor and on the end furthest from the cottage there was an earth closet with two sizes of seat. The closet had a small door half way up the end wall through which ashes were deposited. The night soil man still emptied this during the war years when we stayed there. We also had a pigsty which I can remember being occupied, and there were always ducks, geese and chickens around. The pigsty was eventually demolished but the stable and earth closet were still in use right up until the cottage was demolished. We never saw a horse in the stable but even so it was useful storage space for coal and logs and a large number of old mineral water crates, both full and empty. The stable door was kept locked on busy days to prevent stolen empty bottles being brought back to the cafe door for the one penny refund. Behind the cottage there stood a stable with a cobbled floor and on the end furthest from the cottage there was an earth closet with two sizes of seat. The closet had a small door half way up the end wall through which ashes were deposited. The night soil man still emptied this during the war years when we stayed there. We also had a pigsty which I can remember

(This page - Sarah Marie & William Valentine Frost c.1920)

being occupied, and there were always ducks, geese and chickens around. The pigsty was eventually demolished but the stable and earth closet were still in use right up until the cottage was demolished. We never saw a horse in the stable but even so it was useful storage space for coal and logs and a large number of old mineral water crates, both full and empty. The stable door was kept locked on busy days to prevent stolen empty bottles being brought back to the cafe door for the one penny refund.

Val Frost with chickens - 1933

On the opposite side of the main road towards town there were two semi-detached houses which were inhabited by farm workers employed at Tommy Marsh's farm (now part of the Park) and beyond them was a small quarry with steep sides known as "The Sand-hole", this was where William grew produce for a business he later set up. Latterly, this area was turned into allotments and there were beehives there too. The plots were rented out to other local people. William travelled to Market regularly by horse and cart to sell the produce he had grown; he also used some of the many old brickyard buildings to stable his horses (and later his cows, when he developed a dairy business).

William and Richard Frost taking produce to Doncaster c.1901

William's younger son, Richard, later took over the dairy side of things and the business relocated to the Beckett Road area under the new name, "Wheatley Dairies." Another of William's sons, Arthur, later moved with his family into the other cottage (now the site of a car park) where he ran his own fruit and vegetable business, delivering all over the local area with the aid of his horse-drawn cart.

William Frost's horse and cart at Sandall brickyard - c.1901

William and Sarah went on to open a small cafe in the back room of the cottage, initially to cater for the fishermen who came and bought tickets to fish in the lake. In 1931, Sarah, on a visit to her family home in Fakenham, sadly passed away and William, rather than live alone, opted to go and live with his unmarried daughter in Wheatley.

My grandfather George and his wife Polly took over the tenancy at Sandall, George giving up his Blacksmith's shop off Wheatley Lane and Polly her general store on Beckett Road. We visited Sandall regularly as a family and so knew the place well before it became a park. George had a small flat-bottomed rowing boat and we loved going out onto the lake with him. I suppose we may even have picked up the rudiments of rowing in those early days.

From left to right - George Frost, Noel Frost, Minnie with husband Tom Crundall.

Lemonade for sale at Sandall

We always seemed to be on the water directly below the cottage so I cannot recall whether the fish ponds were still separate then. There were a pair of swans living on the lake - we named the male Jock and he was very large and extremely fierce, needless to say that we soon learned to keep our distance, he had broken a man's arm (allegedly). Sadly, his mate was killed by a fox while she was trapped in the ice one winter but Jock stayed on the lake alone for many years after.

Under the 'new management', the new cafe was expanded. The little back room became a tea-room containing three small tables and my grandfather had his chair in there, next to the fire in winter. He always sat outside in the warmer weather, presiding over proceedings though not taking any part in them. A tea-garden was laid out at the side of the cottage with large wood-topped tables and benches and that area was extremely popular during the summer months.

Orders were taken at the door before trays complete with teapot, milk jug and crockery were carried out into the garden - no disposable ware in those days - there must have been an awful lot of washing up with which we were all expected to help with. Walls ice cream and fizzy drinks were very popular with families too. Winter saw a lot of passing trade from lorry drivers who could buy cigarettes together with tea and sandwiches. There was still only a cold water tap in the kitchen area (the outside pump had gone), and there was no electricity or hot water. A huge black kettle constantly boiled water on the range in the back room where the fire had to be 'kept in' no matter how warm the weather was. Unfortunately, the selling of ice cream stopped abruptly when Massarella's were granted a concession for one of their carts inside the park gates.

Val, cousin Wendy, and Peg - Sandall lakeside, 1939

Our grandmother Polly passed away in 1937 and the running of the cafe became a real problem. Eventually a live-in housekeeper was found to take over the house and cafe combined. The lady was a local widow with grown-up children and grandchildren. It was during the school summer holidays, while she was taking a long break with her family that we began to stay there.

The Park came into being sometime during 1940 while my father was away with the R.A.F. and it was from then that my mother was able to take over. We loved living there and it was so different from our home at Intake. The fact that there was no electricity, no hot water, and only oil lamps at night made the place more exciting for us at least, although it must have been hard work for my mother. We all went home to Intake once a week for baths!
We had our own names for different parts of the park which was much wilder and more overgrown in those days. The area on the far side of the lake where the path rose up was called the "top piece" and at that time did not extend all the way across to Barnby Dun Road as it does today. There was a thick hawthorn hedge along the path which formed the boundary. The remains of that hedge can still be seen in a spaced row of hawthorn trees. As far as I now, the field beyond that belonged to the farm. What is now a wet area and once house the children's boating lake was also part of Tommy Marsh's farm, and was a fish pond. Some of the old farm buildings are still present today.
Before the advent of war stopped work, the council had begun to excavate a circular area opposite the main gate (which at a later stage became a putting green), we understood that a band-stand, similar to that at Hexthorpe Flatts was planned, and huge holes were dug. A flight of about a dozen concrete steps, each about four yards wide, was installed leading down into one of the holes, with giant stone slabs at either side. These steps lead nowhere all through the war years but we made very good use of them as children by inventing a series of games to be played on them.

The coming of the boats to the lake was a very exciting time for us and the fact that we already had some idea how to row from our time spent on grandad's boat was a big positive for us. We must have been a frustration for the boatman because, of course, we were still around when everyone had gone home. Thankfully he was a very good-natured man and he even allowed us to help him. For overnight safety, all the boats, large and small, were tied up

over on the island which was directly opposite the boathouse, and we were allowed to help with that too. Most of the boats were floated across and when most of them were securely tied up, just one small boat was rowed back, lifted out of the water, and locked away inside the boathouse. The whole routine was reversed in the morning and we loved it.

Early boats on the lake

One winter, possible 1947, the lake froze sufficiently for skating to be allowed which drew large crowds. Few people could skate, and even fewer owned a pair of skates, but that didn't seem to matter. Mum and Dad took us down and then helped with the serving of hot soup from the front of the boathouse. At that time, the park had a lot of green folding metal chairs which had a metal bar connecting the bottom of the front legs to the back ones on either side. These chairs were found to be ideal for pushing small children, or the older generation around the ice. It was great fun.

At some point during the war a number of large brick buildings were erected on the high ground to the right of, and above the path leading to the boathouse. I believe that they may have been kitchens for mass catering but I don't think they were ever used. I cannot recall when they were demolished and many people don't seem to remember them at all. My father's cousin, Flo, had a picture of her father, Arthur, who lived in the other cottage, standing with these buildings in the background and I kick myself now for at the time I failed to ask her anything about them.

During the latter years of the war, the Canadian Air Force used the Tote building (which is still there, between the end of the Park and the Wheatley Hotel) to house a succession of their bomber crews who were in transit to the Far East. On many evenings, when the park and cafe were officially closed, some of the officers would stroll down the road in search of a cup of tea, and probably to relieve the boredom. My mother would have to revive the dying fire so as to be able to boil the huge black kettle once more to make their drinks. Imagine running a cafe with only cold water on tap, no electricity and only an open fire! Although we were only children - the eldest of us being around 12 years old - those Canadians were very friendly and we were always very sorry when they moved on. Two of them signed an autograph book with their names and addresses - both were from Ontario -sadly I lost the book but we often wondered if they made it to Burma and then got back to Canada safely, I do hope so.

As the war ended, with my father back at home with us and a new baby in the family, our summer stays there ended, although we still visited every week without fail. By then, we were all older, and the distinct lack of amenities might not have seemed so good. My grandfather still had his housekeeper; in fact, she stayed with him until he died in his sleep in 1956. Within a very short time the cottage had been demolished. We would have liked to have taken photographs but it was gone before we had the chance. Seeing a blank space where once we had spent so many happy times was awful, and we were even more upset when the lovely old cottage was replaced by a very ordinary modern building for the new cafe. I often wonder what happened to the lovely polished mahogany board ceiling when demolition took place. We all slept on camp-beds in that room, and again, the memory of the oil lamp reflecting in that ceiling will never leave my mind.

Florence Frost and family outside the cottage long before demolition. The building was demolished which led to the construction of the new, rather drab, looking café.

Chapter Four

-oOo-

The Storm before the Calm

And so, we have established the fact that Sandall Park has its roots entwined most firmly around and within the history and heritage of Doncaster, from medieval farming, through pre and post Victorian industry, before finally meeting the Great War era as a market garden supplying fresh produce to the town. From this time onwards Sandall had to experience growing pains and teething problems as it negotiated its transition into the much loved park that we see before us today. We are thankful indeed that the story does not end badly and there certainly was a halcyon 'middle-age' to the site. We move now into the memories that still live in the thoughts and minds of townsfolk that are still with us. During the early weeks of 2014 I made a request for information on a popular social networking website and was amazed at the quantity of the responses I received. Few could recount and compile their memories into more than half of a page or so, but everyone could form a sentence of happy and positive memories of picnics in the park, rowing the hired boats on the lake, eating ice-creams under the shade of the ancient oak trees, or feeding the ducks, geese, or the famous black swans that populated the water.

The focus of attention seems to be on the boats that one could hire and take out on the lake. Whether that is because that was the visitor's favourite aspect or whether that was the sole attraction is unclear, however, whatever the reason it is the main thing that seems to be stored in people's minds. The boats arrived in the 1940's as Margaret Frost informed us in her earlier chapter and although there were only a handful of second-hand vessels available back then, from that point on nearly every photographs has the boating lake as its subject. The earliest photograph in my collection is the one at the end of the previous chapter where I estimate the era to be the late 1950's to early 1960's. I am convinced there must exist earlier photographs but I have not seen them with my own eyes.

The 'famous' boathouse at Sandall Park c.1980

The boathouse at Sandall Park became a local landmark and something that was instantly recognizable on every picture, postcard and greetings card that was ever created. It was by no means an architectural statement but it was however, fit for purpose. Images of it are not rare by any stretch of the imagination and I am certain you will all have seen versions of the above photograph at some time or another. The whole shape and layout of the park is still the same as it ever was so that although vast improvements have been to the fabric of the place, were an individual who knew the park well during the 1970's and 80's to pay another visit in 2014, they would have no problem finding their way around.

This now and then photograph demonstrates that fact quite well with the sweep of the banks, the island in the centre of the lake and the shelter at the far side having undergone no changes whatsoever.

Many of the people I approached for their memories also spoke of the 'little train' and the pitch and putt golf course. One of these individuals was a lady named Sheena Ballard who held many fond memories of the park, not only from her own childhood but from taking others to visit it. She remarked, "I have known the Park for most of my life and thought you may be interested in some of my recollections.

I lived in Wheatley throughout my childhood and so Grove Park was the nearest recreational area. It was a good place, offering entertainment on the putting green, in the playground, running up and down the steps to the bowling green, the tennis courts and the hope of seeing the 'mad woman' who lived in the big house adjoining. It could not, however, deliver the same expectation of thrills and excitement as the Boating Lake, a mile along the road. I didn't realise it was actually called Sandall Park until years later.

As a child of 6 and 7 I would beg my mother to take me to the Boating Lake rather than Grove Park. It was a mile further away, and to little legs it seemed a good deal further. My mum's housekeeping money could stretch to either the bus fare to get there, or half an hour on the boats (I seem to recall it was 6d for half an hour, 9d for an hour). There was no contest – I walked both ways without a murmur to get that magical time in a boat. There were smaller boats to seat 4 and larger ones for 6 or 8 people – I always chose the smaller because the big ones were too heavy for me to row. My mum used to try to persuade me to go on the pedaloes on the small children's lake but I wouldn't – the pull of circumnavigating the islands on the big lake, being hidden from the view of the boat man, was too great to sacrifice.

The Dell opposite the children's boating lake where picnics were enjoyed

I recall the thrill of being allowed to walk up to the Boating Lake with a friend for the first time. We used to make rafts from ice lolly sticks to float on the lake, play on the swings and if we could afford it go on a boat. And, of course, run up and down the wall of the steps leading from the lakeside to the football pitches making our own games to see who got to the top first. During school holidays we spent hours there, taking sandwiches so we didn't have to go home until teatime. There was a small dell opposite the entrance to the children's boating pool with trees that were great for sitting in – many picnics were taken there.

My mum and elder sister often went to the Park to play pitch and putt. I was allowed to carry their putters when not in use. I still recall the excitement of being allowed to drive the ball for the first time from a tee – I would like to say that it was discovered I had natural talent and went on to great things in the golfing world but sadly not – I did enjoy playing there for several years though. I recall the Peter Pan train being near the pitch and putt, as in the photo, but can't remember when it appeared.

Time passed and in my late teens I started to take my young nephews to the Boating Lake. They enjoyed it as much as I had done – duck feeding, swinging, playing on the steps and going on the putting green. I visited the Park regularly to dog walk, always enjoying the autumn most when the ground was covered in leaves.

When I married I moved to Wheatley Hills and lived only 5 minutes from the park. When my daughter arrived we went there for a walk every day. As she began to toddle it was as though the intervening years had never happened – duck feeding, playing on the steps, the playground (by then revamped and far better for it) – timeless activities unblemished by passing time. If only the boats had still been there. In sad times which inevitably happen to all of us on occasion I always went to the Park to think. Walking round the lake always seemed to put things in perspective.

My daughter is now grown and I live 15 miles from Sandall Park, so rarely get the opportunity to visit. However, on the occasions that I have been in the last 2 or 3 years it is apparent that the Friends of Sandall Park are trying to make it an enduring facility that will continue to give pleasure to future generations. I do hope so."

This page, Sheena, Sandall Park - 1973

Sheena enjoying some family time at the park c.1981

Chapter Five

-oOo-

The fall from Grace

After some six decades of public enjoyment of this little corner of Doncaster, the park that we knew and loved so well was to enter a period of doom and gloom. More than that, it was to become a derelict and neglected place that no-one of sane mind would have been proud of, let alone visit. Like a delinquent child in need of foster parents there was little hope for Sandall Park ever finding a responsible guardian to care of its needs. The pleasant greenery became a jungle and the neatly planted leylandii hedgerows that once quelled the winds attempting to race across the pitch and putt now reached for the stars and served only to block the tired park from public view. Behind these hedges took place the most criminal of activities so that the whole park became a den of iniquity and a popular haunt for those members of our society wishing to engage in what we now call 'anti-social behaviour'.

By way of contrast we must first visit the park during the darkest of its hour's, in order for us to truly appreciate the colossal task that had to be undertaken so that Sandall Park might once again become an asset rather than a failure. During the year 1994, a series of photographs were taken which document the state of the park before 'The Friends' were ever on the scene. These photographs (now twenty years old), show a park that is almost unrecognisable when compared to what we see today, however, they served as a good benchmark. They certainly were a great starting point for improvements; let's face it, any changes for the betterment of Sandall Park would have been welcomed.

The former council depot became a magnet for vandalism

The main car park was in a sorry state, full of potholes and extremely dirty

The rear of the council depot was a real eyesore creating completely the wrong impression

The path leading to the toilet block and the main car park was very private and enclosed

Scenes such as this one were a commonplace. Motorbikes were ridden illegally within the park, and stolen ones left to rot having been set alight behind the cover of the tall trees. Drinks parties were commonplace and no manmade addition to the park was left untouched. Benches were vandalized and graffiti covered every surface that could be sprayed, scratched or painted. Litter was just dropped for the next person to pick up and fly-tipping was a huge problem. The toilet block was a disgrace and on the verge of being decommissioned forever. The main car park became the meeting place for criminals and undesirables and the wildfowl became a target for certain warped individuals to take out their frustrations on.

In 2003 a group was formed, the predecessor of the Friends of Sandall Park. With all the best intentions this group had underestimated just how much needed to be done to bring the park back to an acceptable standard. After all, it was not just a case of rebuilding and repairing, it was a case of educating, policing, supervising and changing the attitudes of a whole generation.

This 2003 formation quickly ceased and was replaced by the Friends of Sandal Park in 2004. In 2005, Don and Sandra Crabtree joined the group and, although they didn't know it at the time, it would from this point forward that real change would be achieved. Don't be fooled though, this new group was faced with the same animosity as the previous one, however, they must have been a hardier and more determined bunch for they persevered through every kind of negative that could be thrown at them.

In April 2005, Sandra Crabtree put out an appeal for old photographs of the park in the local newspaper in an effort to enable the public to both remember what a lovely place Sandall used to be and to gauge how much interest there still existed. On September 15th of the same year the official website was launched to keep people up to date with efforts to improve the park and create a better environment, followed by a feature in the local 'Roundabout', St. Aiden's parish church magazine which read,

'The Friends of Sandall Park wish to announce their recently launched website at www.sandallpark.org.uk, check it out and see what's happening! The Friends of Sandall Park (FOSP) is a group of like-minded people - volunteers and official - working towards creating a better environment for the local community within Sandall Park (known locally as 'The Boating Lake) at Wheatley, in Doncaster. The group, originally set up two years ago has been reformed with a new team of people who are committed to improving the park and more recently, with a new chairman taking the helm. Their plans have been incorporated into an ambitious business plan which will develop over a few years to provide the community and visitors with a facility to be proud of. If you are keen, committed and enthusiastic, and have some time to spare, you may be interested in joining the Friends of Sandall Park.'

Such a statement shows a real level of commitment! They really were starting as they meant to go on. There were activities of every kind organised to rally interest in the park and money needed to be raised too. Around one year after the Crabtree's joined the group it was becoming very clear that something drastic was needed if Sandall was ever to be turned around. The Doncaster Advertiser of 1st September, 2006 carried the headline - "BRING BACK WARDENS IN OUR PARKS." The article was a plea from FOSP and other campaigners who were tired and sickened of "sick thugs enticing ducks and geese out of the fishing lake only to shoot them with air rifles after they've kicked them around on the turf." In July 2006, warden patrols had ceased in Sandall Park leading to an alarming increase in vandalism, damage and anti-social behaviour.

FRIENDS OF SANDALL PARK

present

Music in the Park

Friends of Sandall Park gratefully acknowledge assistance given by Community First in this project

on

Saturday, 17th June, 2006

Gates open at 4 p.m.
Concert from 6·30 p.m. to 9 p.m.

Enjoy a relaxed evening in Sandall Park listening to a selection of Big Band music from two extremely talented youth bands. Bring your picnic, rugs, chairs if you wish. We regret no barbecues or gazebos.

FREE Admission
FREE Parking

Car Park entrance on Barnby Dun Road, opposite Stoneacre Car Showroom

This event is sponsored by Wheatley Area Community Partnership Pioneer Fund

featuring
the internationally
renowned and award
winning

Doncaster Youth Swing Orchestra

Directed by John S. M. Ellis, MBE

and

EKS Big Band

from Doncaster's twin town Herten in Germany
Directed by Thomas Vennes

Enquiries to
07967 212720

www.sandallpark.org.uk

A little over 6 weeks later the Doncaster Free Press reported, "DISABLED MAN KICKED IN HEAD BY PARK THUGS. The man was pushed to the ground and kicked by a gang of teenagers as he walked through Sandall Park with his 11 year old son."

These cases are just two of many; in fact, there was a negative report in the local press at least once every month! Did this discourage the FOSP from their aims and aspirations? No, during the summer months of 2006 a musical extravaganza was held called 'Music in the Park.' One review said of it, "Thanks to the Friends of Sandall Park who organised some fine weather as well as candy floss and a row of portaloo's, our evening of music in the park was a fine success. It took us back to all those long, lazy days of summer that we remember having in the past, but are far too busy to find time for nowadays: a rare treat. While families picnicked on the grass, took leisurely summer strolls and had a nice relaxing sprawl, energetic kids and dogs had plenty of space to romp and play in safety around the edges."

As summer turned to autumn and winter set in, Christmas was soon over and 2007 arrived in a manner that FOSP had become all too well accustomed to, yet more vandalism at the park! In an effort to make the park more aesthetically pleasing a whole raft of new planting had been undertaken, with fresh colourful bedding plants and shrubs so pleasing to the eye. Imagine the anger and frustration when the plants were quickly pulled up and thrown into the lake nearby. It was the fourth time in four months that vandals had targeted areas that had been improved by volunteers and some members were left feeling so deflated that they "really did think about giving up, but then that would be admitting that these young vandals had won." This story had a happy ending as a team of police divers who were due to undergo training at Sandall Park came to the rescue, diving for the plants and fishing them out of the water.

I cannot quite put my finger on it, but from this point on something changed. It was as if these sad events were a great turning point, a catalyst, a crossroads from where the FOSP could either throw the towel in or meet the vandals head on. Thankfully, it was the latter for from this point on the positives far outweigh the negatives. The Music in the Park event that had proved so popular in 2006 was once again held to even greater success. The group received over £1100 in donations and the reviews were excellent. In 2008 a new nature trail was launched which included 40 bird boxes, plants, shrubs and trees, wildlife boards and a new picnic area with benches and footpaths. Three 'Fitness Trails' were introduced as a further way to encourage members of the community to return to the park, and members of the public were invited to join in a series of three walks along each of the three routes to mark the official launch.

3

SANDALL PARK
DONCASTER

Sandall Park has three fitness trails of varying lengths, one of which is suitable for the less able and pushchair users. A guide is available which estimates the amount of calories burned on each trail. The Friends of Sandall Park have also installed fitness equipment that can be used in a variety of ways, providing an alternative to the gym.

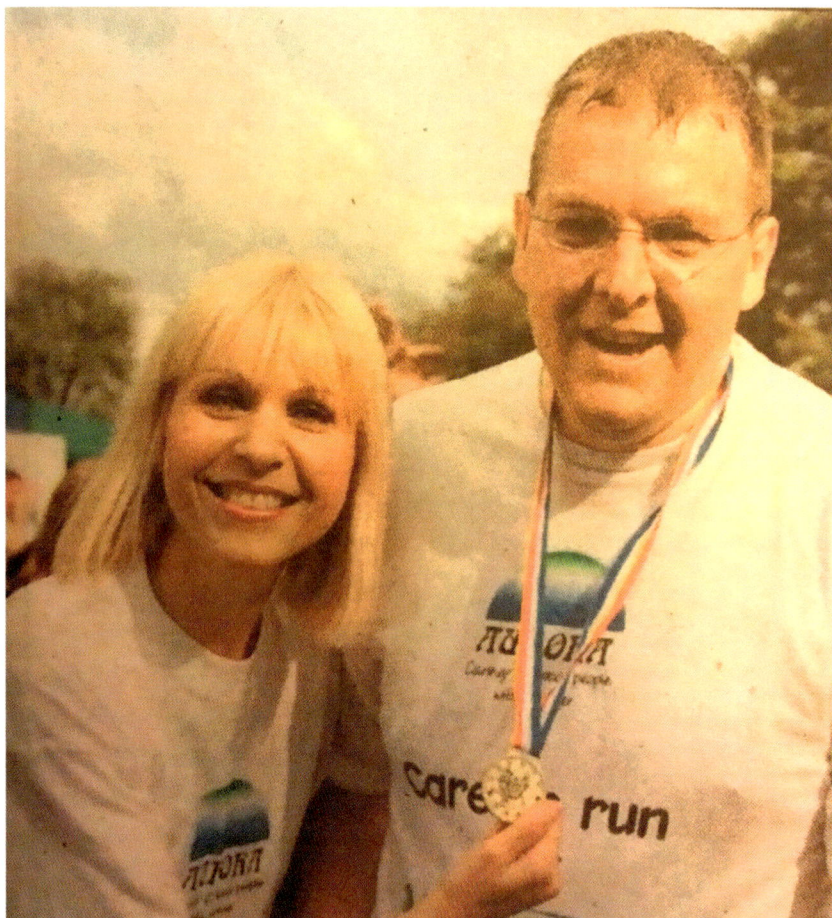

In 2009, on Sunday 7th September a large and well attended charity event was organised for the benefit of that local cancer charity 'Aurora'. The event took the form of a run which saw competitors taking on 2 laps of the whole park. It was extremely well attended with over 800 members of the public taking part including ITV's Calendar presenter Carolyn Hodgson. The event also marked the culmination of a long project to transform the former pitch and putt golf course at the park facilitated by means of a £20,000 grant from the Groundwork charity. The ITV presenter was not only on hand to distribute medals to the runners but also to officially open the new area which was created as an open space for families to enjoy. Also added, was an outdoor gym consisting of hard-wearing steel equipment.

Since time immemorial, the Friends of Sandall Park have been raising awareness of their good cause and helping local charities into the bargain and long may it continue. Events are held all year round from volunteer days to large scale concerts. The Friends really are turning the tables in creating a good name for themselves and an even better one for the park.

Above - **Carolyn Hodgson presents a well earned medal to Darren Burke of the Free Press**

Conclusion

-oOo-

Hard Work Pays Dividends

March 2011 saw the Friends being chosen for a four page article in the national Saga magazine. The article gave a brief history of the park, from its early creation to its sad demise around the millennium. The feature provides the definitive explanation as to why the park is going from strength to strength today. During an interview Don Crabtree remarked, "Everything we do we consider how much of a target it is for criminals." I think this sums up the predicament perfectly. The vandals and criminals haven't stopped visiting the park; they are just extremely limited as to how much damage they can do. When Don Crabtree was drafted in he already had a wealth of experience in reducing crime and tackling anti-social behaviours. He knew that until those issues were properly addressed the positive work of the Friends group would always come to very little, or nothing at all. With Don's valued experience and Sandra's law enforcement background, together with the help and support of the other members they slowly turned the fate of the park around. Every aspect of Sandall Parks arrangement has been carefully thought out so as to minimize its liability, from the placement of new features to the removal of hedgerows, the whole park has been transformed into a place of enjoyment and security for all to enjoy.

A truce was made between the 'Friends' and the fishermen who frequented the lake which allowed night fishing to take place at the park. The arrangement sees the fishermen acting as night security guards protecting the area from vandalism and antisocial behaviour. All in all the ongoing work at the park is paying dividends. The pure commitment and passion from the Friends of Sandall Park is creating a safe haven for both the community and wildlife right in the centre of urban and industrial development. There is no let-up and there seems to be no end to the achievements of the Friends. Every year there are events planned to entertain children of all ages and families of every demographic. Events cater for every budget and raise invaluable funds for both the working group and other nominated charities. If there was ever a model to base a successful community group on then The Friends of Sandall Park are it.

The Little Train - c. 1970 © Alison Vainlo 2014

The Little Train - c. 1970 © Alison Vainlo 2014

The Little Train - c. 1970 © Alison Vainlo 2014

"Come in number 16"

L-R, Sandra Crabtree, Rt. Hon Rosie Winterton, Don Crabtree, Wendy Jenkins from Groundforce UK. © Don Crabtree 2014

New Book Available NOW in All Good Bookshops

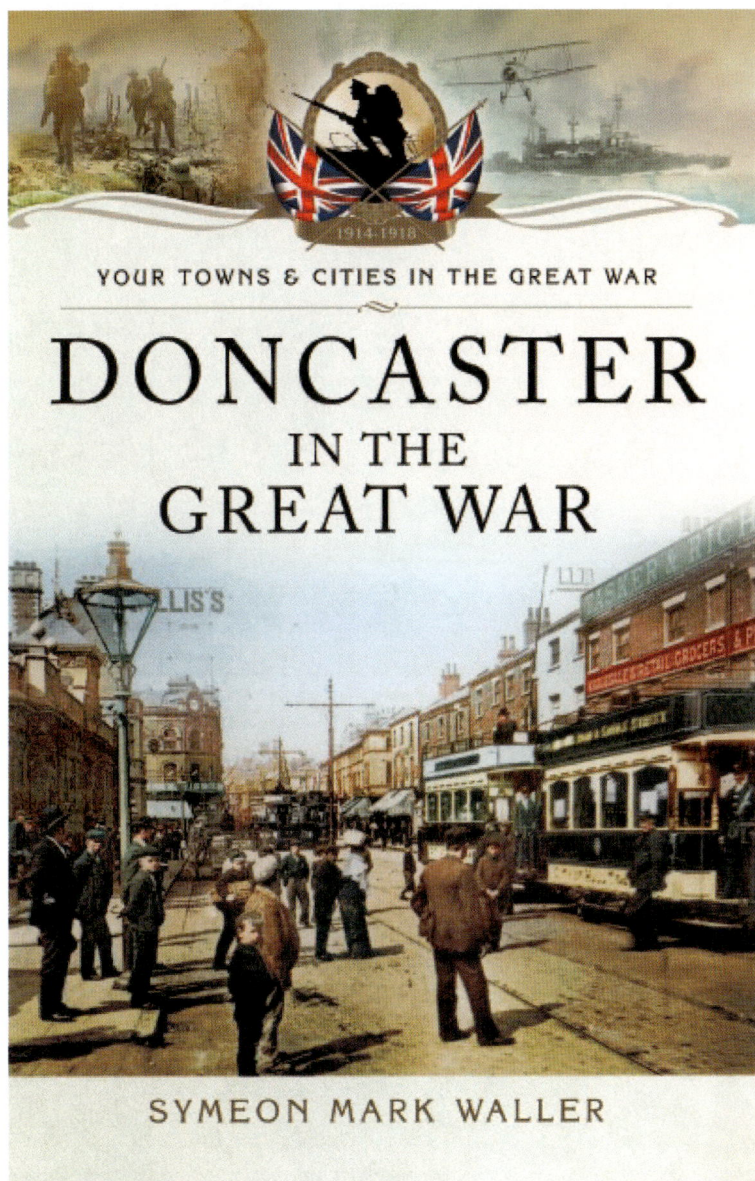

YOUR TOWNS & CITIES IN THE GREAT WAR

DONCASTER
IN THE
GREAT WAR

SYMEON MARK WALLER

Made in the USA
Charleston, SC
10 August 2015